Mel Bay Presents

UPBEAT
SCALES &
ARPEGGIOS

Avrahm Galper Clarinet Series

1 2 3 4 5 6 7 8 9 0

Visit us on the Web at www.melbay.com — E-mail us at email@melbay.com

CONTENTS

PREFACE

Imagine how wonderful it would feel to play everything on your clarinet with confidence and ease. By practicing the scales and arpeggios in this book you can achieve such mastery.

The studies in this book evolved from the Baermann Scale studies. For impetus and melodic direction, I begin each exercise on the upbeat. Moreover, I wrote the studies using eighth notes in Alla Breve so that you can play at your own pace.

All the studies are re-ordered from the original to a more logical sequence, staying within a given key for each exercise. They cover a broad range of musical forms including simple, interrupted and returning scales; major, minor and broken chords; dominant sevenths, thirds and sixths; fifths and octaves and diminished sevenths.

And I've included many diagrams to help you learn new fingerings, including some that are not commonly known.

David Blumberg, Adjunct Clarinet Instructor, University of Pennsylvania, has observed that the upbeat approach I take in this book is similar to the 2341 method used by Marcel Tabuteau of the Curtis Institute. This method gives direction to each musical phrase.

By mastering the studies in this book you will be able to handle many musical challenges that come your way. If your goal is to improve your clarinet playing - and I know it is - this book will be an invaluable guide.

Avrahm Galper
Toronto, Canada

ABOUT THE AUTHOR

Internationally known and respected, Avrahm "Abe" Galper was principal clarinetist with the Toronto Symphony for 30 years. Mr. Galper also served as principal clarinetist with the Palestine Opera Company, the Israel Philharmonic, the C.B.C. Symphony, the Toronto Philharmonic, and the Canadian Opera Company.

Galper has played under conductors Andrew Davis, Karl Ancerl, Seiji Ozawa, Walter Susskind, Sir Ernest Macmillan, John Barbirolli, Pierre Monteaux, Colin Davis, Efrem Kurtz, Charles Munch, Leopold Stokowski, and many others.

He has taught at the Indiana University at Bloomington. He has also given master classes in Beijing and Shanghai, China. He was clarinet consultant to the Claude Watson School of Arts in Toronto. He is currently a member of the Music Faculty at the University of Toronto and a member of the Faculty of the Glenn Gould Professional School of Music at the Royal Conservatory of Music in Toronto.

Mr. Galper first studied with Tzvi Tzipine in Palestine, later with Frederic Thurston at the Royal College of Music in London. In New York he studied with Simeon Bellison of the New York Philharmonic.

Now through his books and inventions, clarinetists of all ages and abilities can benefit from Mr. Galper's experience as a professional clarinetist and teacher of clarinet.

10 TIPS FOR SUCCESSFUL PRACTICING

1. Set up a daily practice schedule and stick to it. Ask your teacher to help you design a practice schedule that's right for you.

2. Know what you want to accomplish during each practice session. It is better to practice for short time well than a long time carelessly.

3. Use good quality reeds and change them often.

4. Keep your fingers curved and close to their respective keys and tone holes.

5. Try to learn as many alternate fingering combinations as you can to help you play more fluently. The fingerings in this book will be of great help.

6. Listen to good clarinet players in concert or recordings to help you acquire a concept of what a beautiful clarinet tone sounds like. Always listen to yourself to make sure that your playing is in time and in tune.

7. A well developed tone in the low register is fundamental to a beautiful clarinet tone.

8. Play with a full sound, making sure the air stream is steady with constant abdominal support.

9. Practice the exercises in this book musically, not mechanically, to help you develop good expression.

10. Approach difficult passages slowly until you get them right. Do not ignore these passages or skip over them. You will master them if you are patient and persistent.

FINGERINGS

Knowing a variety of fingerings is like having a good vocabulary. You can express yourself in many ways. In this book, I frequently provide suggested fingerings for a given note above and below the staff. While the bottom fingering is most often used, you should try to learn the topfingering, as well. It might be more suitable for you. Or it might be useful in a future technical passage.

Here is an explanation of the fingering symbols that I use in this book.

BASIC FINGERING SYMBOLS

The letter "R" means that you should use the right hand fingering for the note.

The letter "L" means you should use the left hand fingering for the note.

The Roman numerals "I," "II," and "III" correspond to the first, second, and third fingers of the hand that plays the notes.

The letter "S" refers to the side key(s).

For instance, if the throat F♯ has an "I" underneath it, finger the note with the first finger of your left hand. However, if the same note has an "S" below it, play the F♯ using the thumb with the lower two trill keys (#7 and #8).

Together ⌐_____⌐
Play the notes above (or below) the symbol 'together'. Use the fingerings indicated.

Leave on ⌐_____
In the transition from C to B, leave the C key depressed while playing B.

Although there are other notes between the first B and C, do not remove your fingers for the intermediate notes.

This is a combination of two Leave Ons.

Slide symbol ▶

While sliding is generally frowned upon, it is sometimes unavoidable. Try to become familiar with sliding patterns like those described above. Remember to keep you fingers relaxed when you slide.

Sometimes it is necessary to slide from B to C♯ with the little finger of the left hand. In the second half of this measure, slide from D♯ to C♯ using the little finger of the right hand.

Here is a similar measure showing the same progression performed with different slides.

In this example, slide the little finger of the right hand from D♯ to C♯.

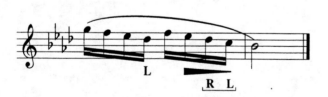

In the descending progression from E♭ to D♭ to C in the second half of this measure, slide the little finger of your right hand from E♭ to C as you depress the D♭ key with your left hand.

Ready - - - - - -

Hold down the fingering for the note at the end of the Symbol while playing the preceding notes.

TAKING BREATHS

Sometimes in an exercise, no natural breathing place is apparent. When you need to take a breath, try the following method:

1. Stop on the first note of a measure.
2. Hold the note for two beats.
3. Take a breath but keep counting to maintain the beat.
4. Make the appropriate entrance, beginning with the note that comes after the one where you left off in step #1

CHROMATIC SCALE

FINGERING CHART

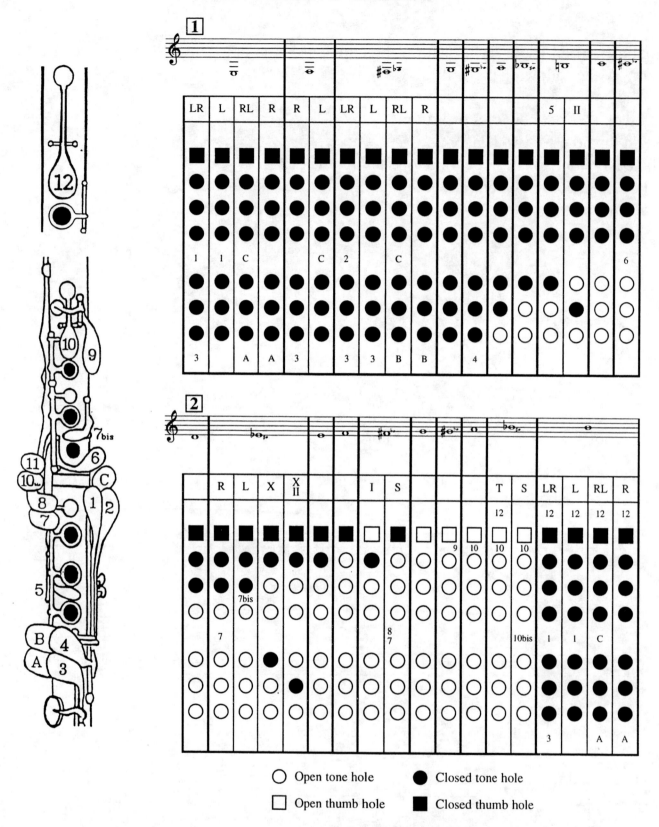

○ Open tone hole   ● Closed tone hole

□ Open thumb hole   ■ Closed thumb hole

R-right hand; L-left hand
I-first finger; II-second finger; III-third finger
S-side key or keys; 5-trill key; X-fork

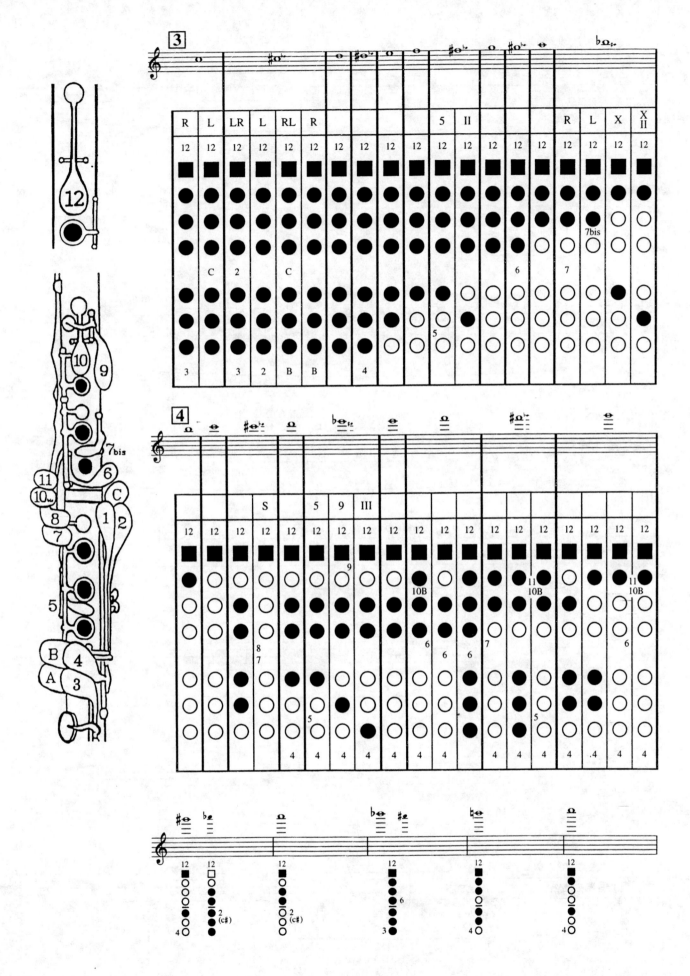

C Major

Broken Chord

Interrupted Scale

Broken Chords

Returning Scales

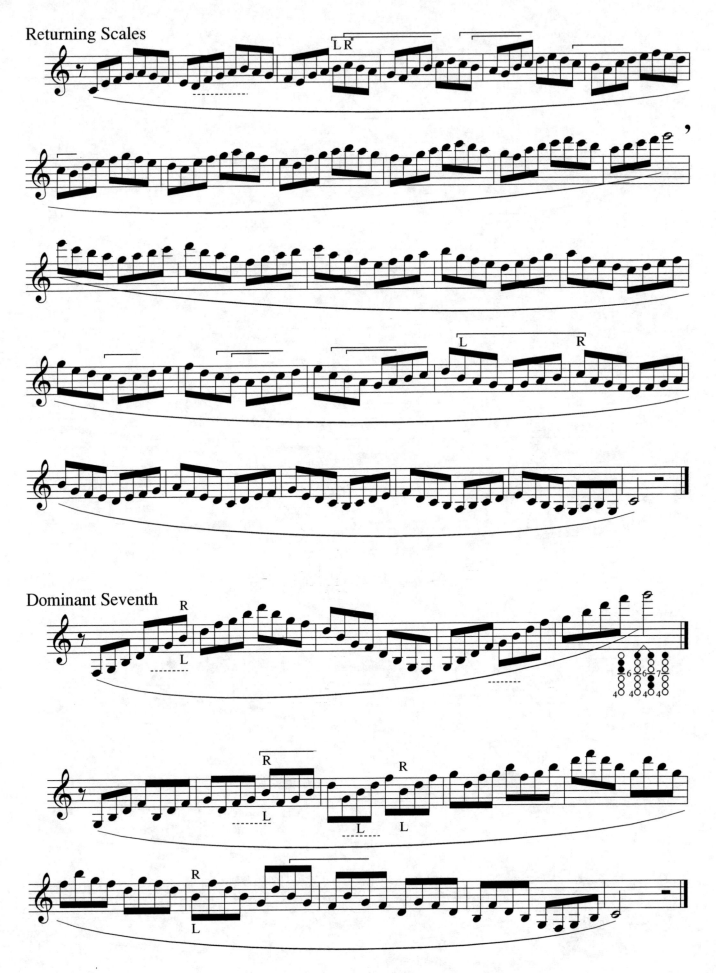

Dominant Seventh

(dominant seventh continued)

Thirds

Sixths

A Minor

Melodic

Harmonic

Broken Chord

Interrupted Scales - Melodic

Harmonic

Broken Chords

Various Chords

Thirds

Sixths

G Major

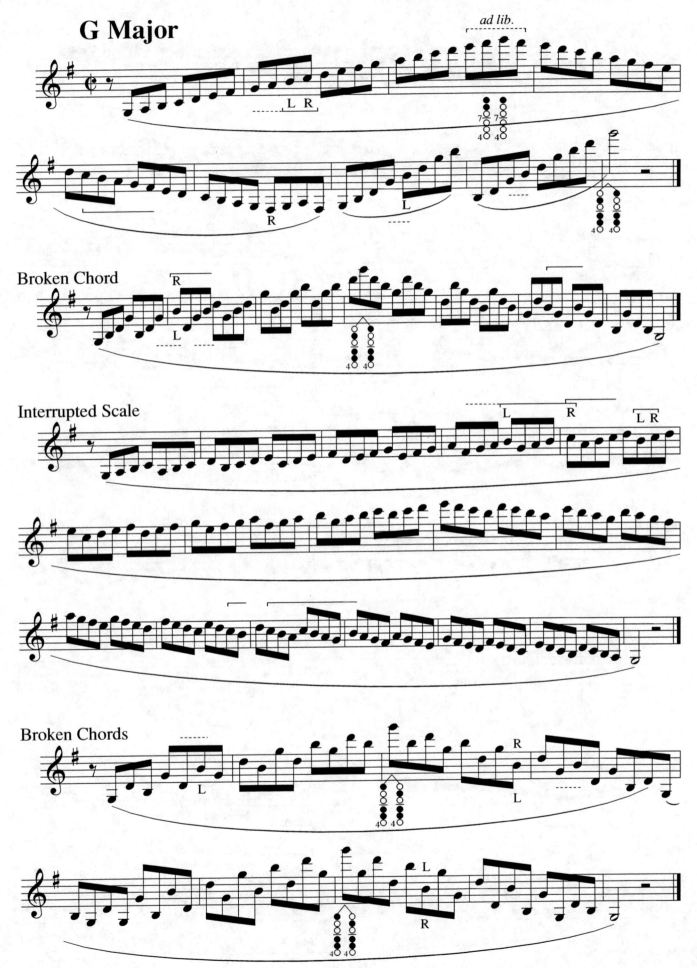

Broken Chord

Interrupted Scale

Broken Chords

15

Returning Scales

Dominant Seventh

(dominant seventh continued)

Thirds

Sixths

17

E Minor

Melodic

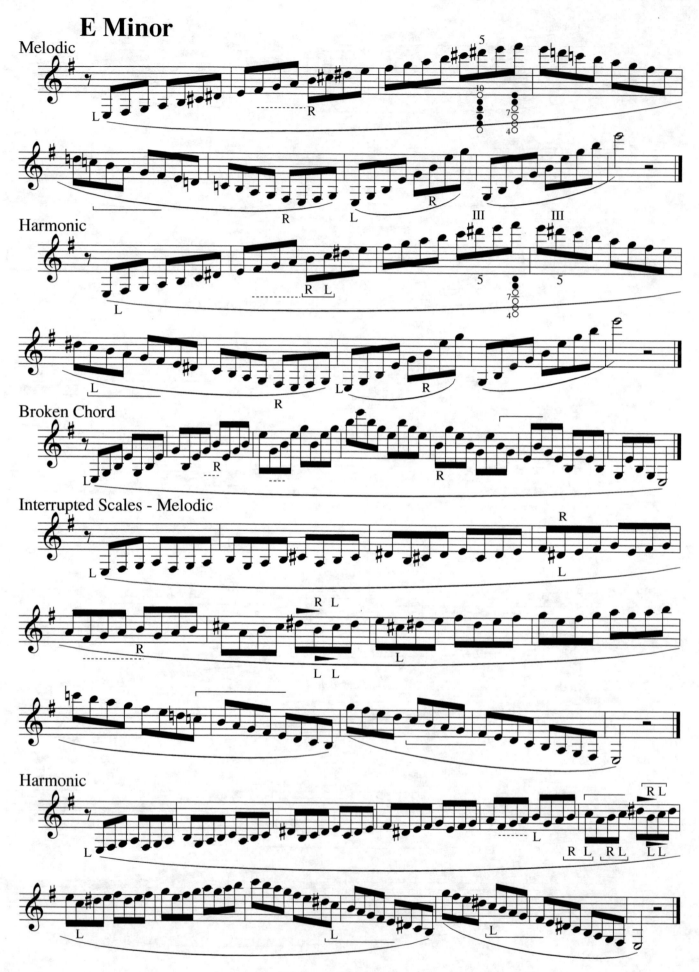

Harmonic

Broken Chord

Interrupted Scales - Melodic

Harmonic

Broken Chords

Various Chords

Thirds

Sixths

19

F Major

Returning Scales

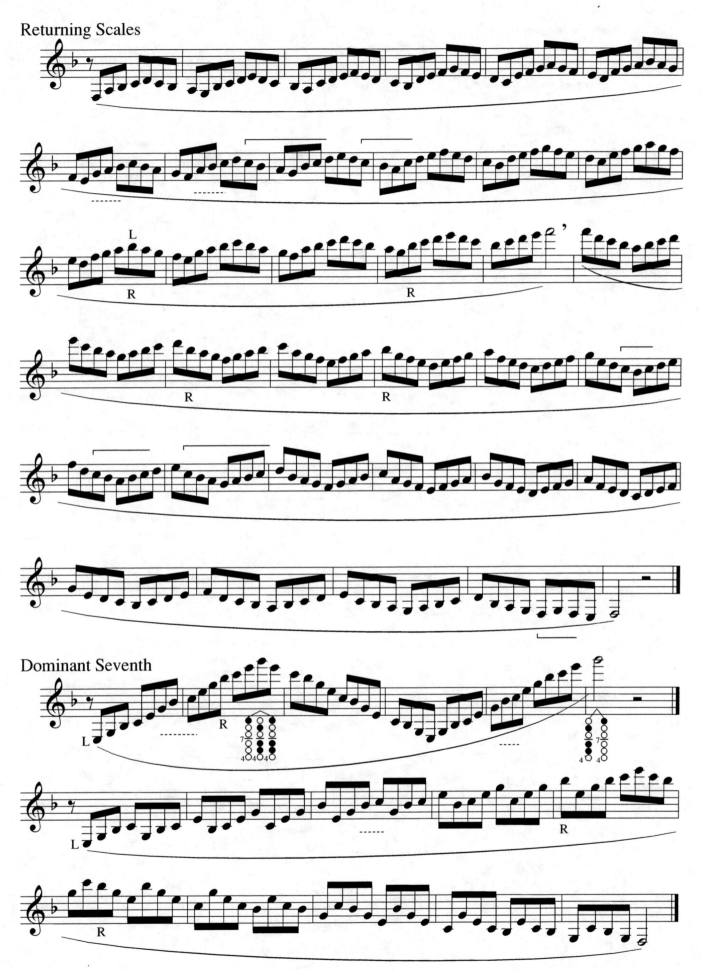

Dominant Seventh

(dominant seventh continued)

Thirds

Sixths

D Minor

Broken Chords

Various Chords

Thirds

Sixths

24

D Major

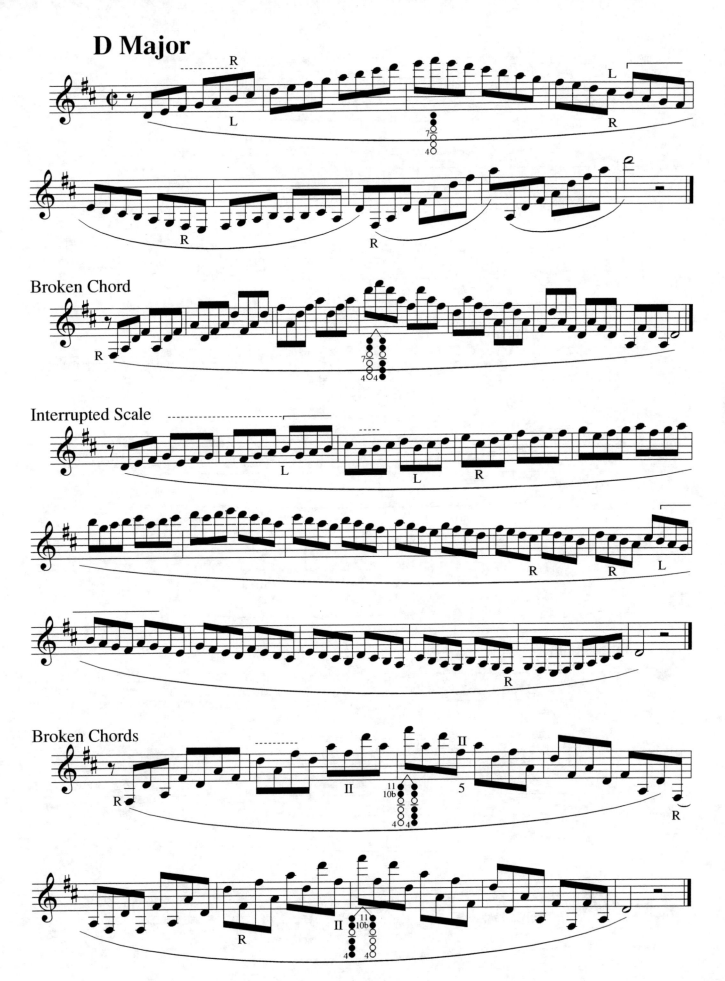

Broken Chord

Interrupted Scale

Broken Chords

Returning Scales

Dominant Seventh

(dominant seventh continued)

Thirds

Sixths

B Minor

Melodic

Harmonic

Broken Chord

Interrupted Scales - Melodic

Harmonic

Broken Chords

Various Chords

Thirds

Sixths

29

B♭ Major

Broken Chord

Interrupted Scale

Broken Chords

30

Returning Scales

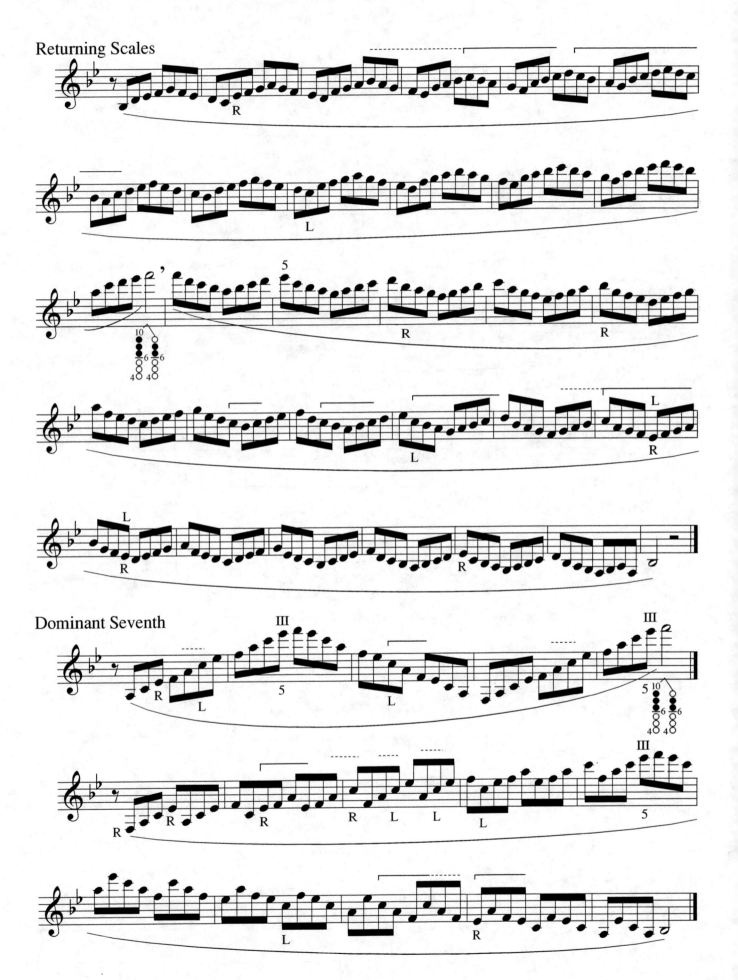

Dominant Seventh

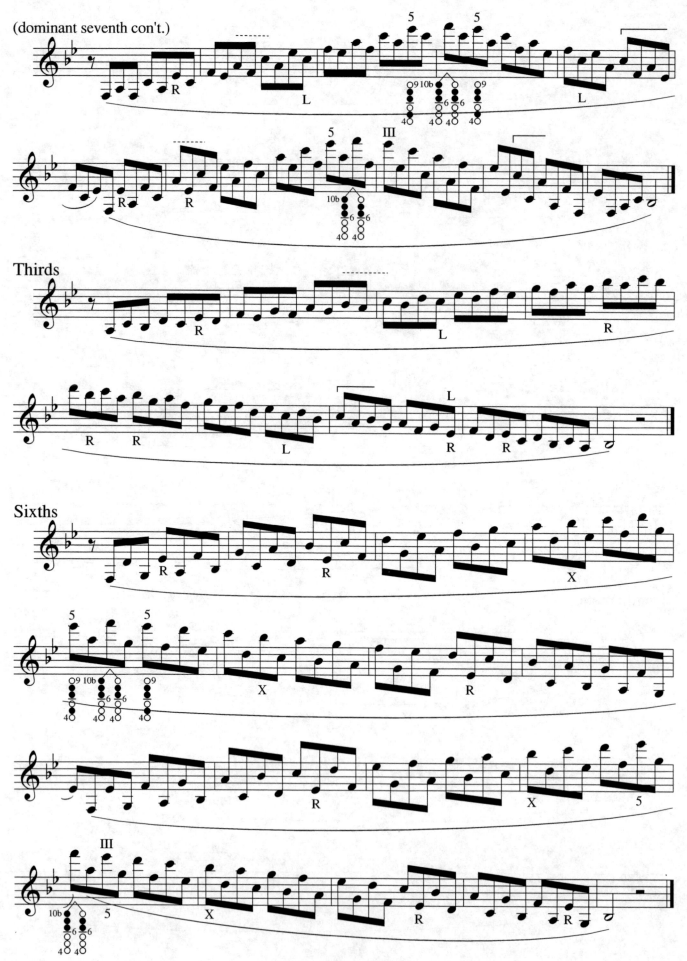

G Minor

Melodic

Harmonic

Broken Chord

Returning Scales - Melodic

Harmonic

Broken Chords

Various Chords

Thirds

Sixths

A Major

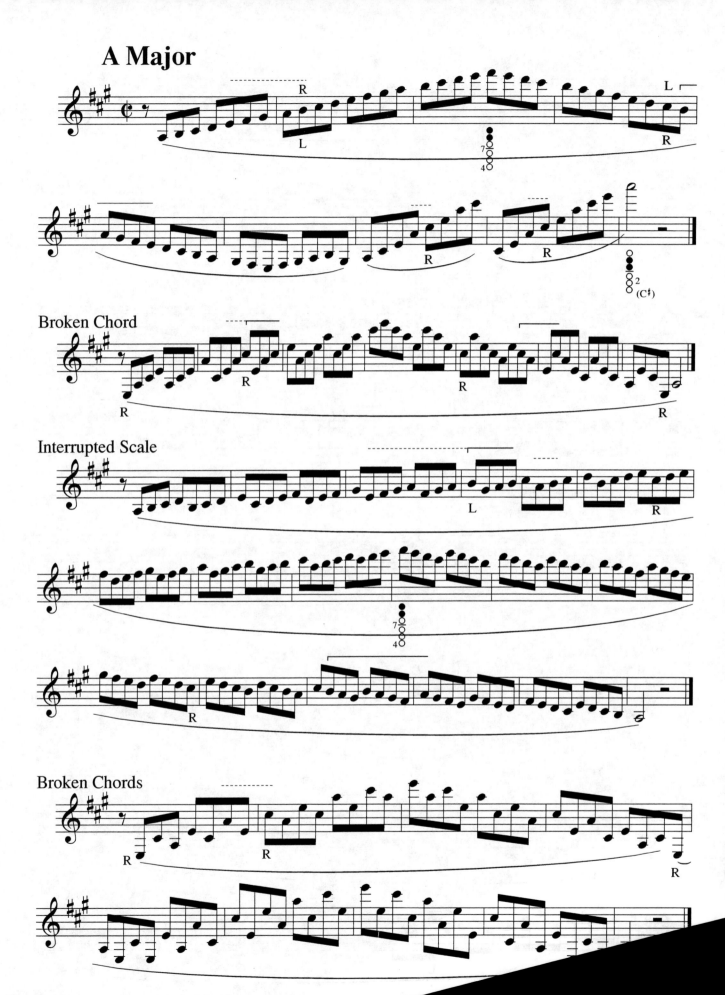

Broken Chord

Interrupted Scale

Broken Chords

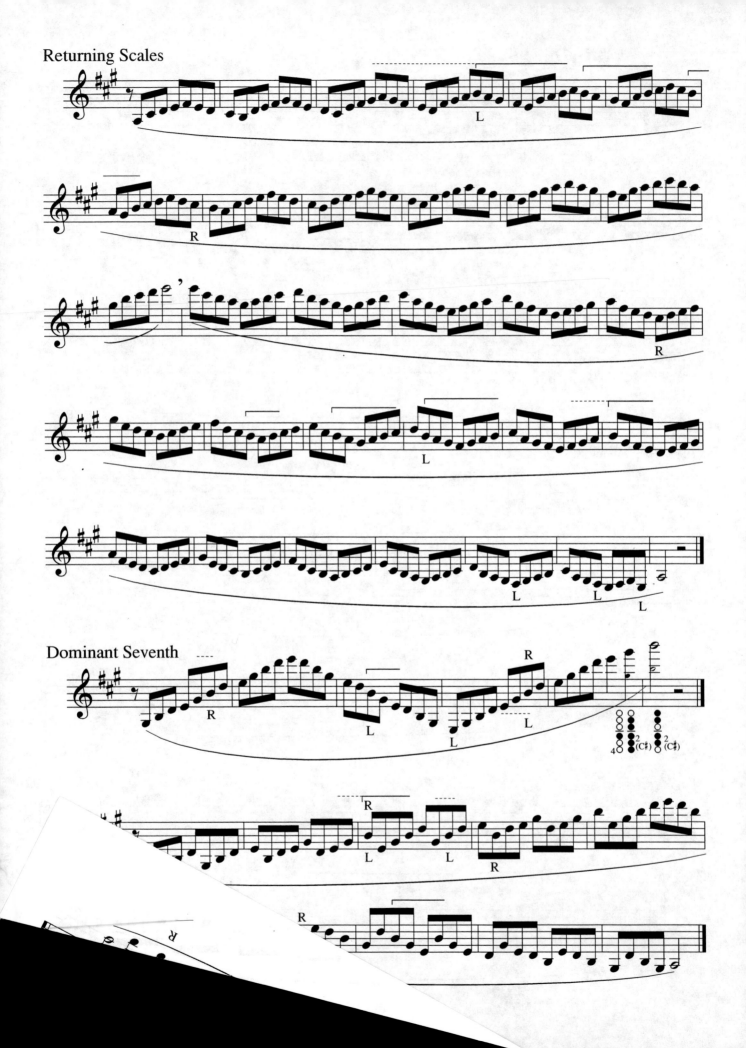

(dominant seventh continued)

Thirds

Sixths

Melodic **F♯ Minor**

37

Harmonic

Broken Chord

Interrputed Scales - Melodic

Harmonic

38

39

E♭ Major

Returning Scales

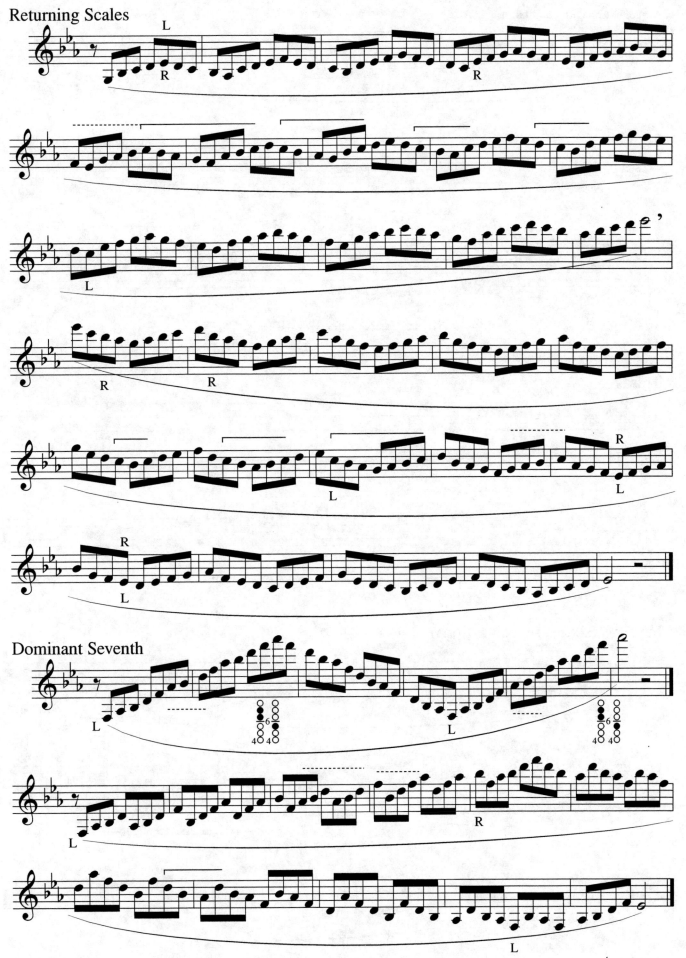

Dominant Seventh

41

(dominant seventh continued)

Thirds

Intervals (sixths, sevenths, fifths)

C Minor

43

44

E Major

Broken Chord

Interrupted Scale

Broken Chords

45

Returning Scales

Dominant Seventh

(dominant seventh continued)

Thirds

Sixths

C# Minor

Melodic

Harmonic

Broken Chord

Interrupted Scales - Melodic

Harmonic

Broken Chords

Various Chords

Thirds

Sixths

49

A♭ Major

Broken Chord

Interrupted Scale

Broken Chords

50

Returning Scales

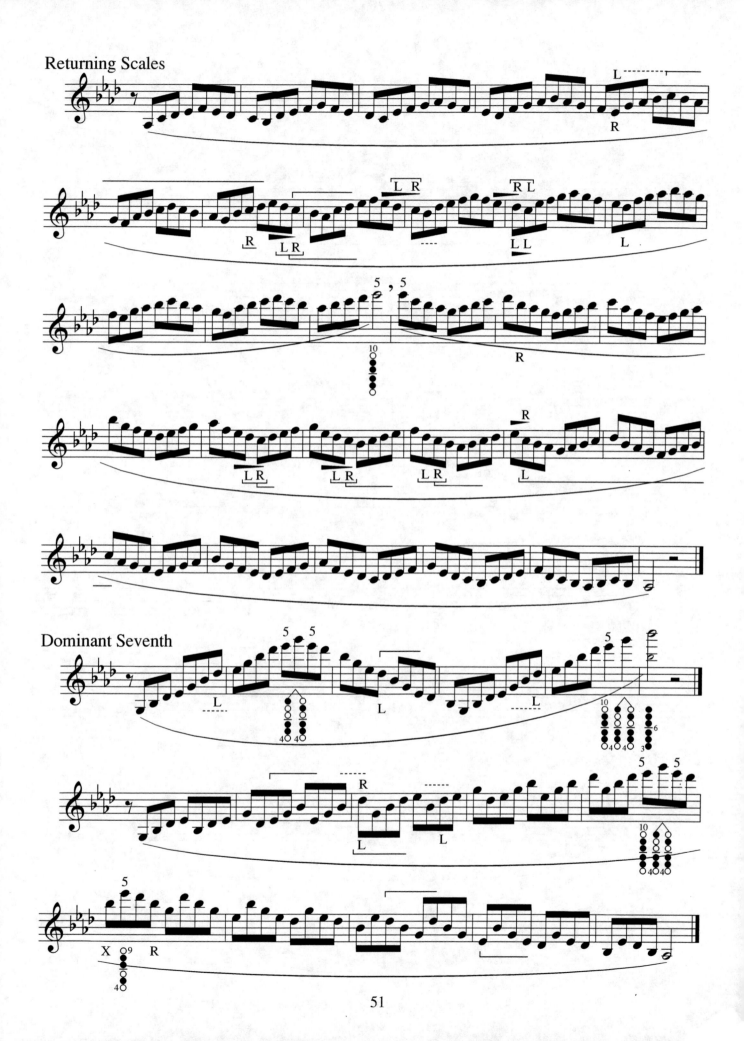

Dominant Seventh

Thirds

Sixths

Melodic **F Minor**

52

Harmonic

Broken Chord

Returning Scales - Melodic

Harmonic

Broken Chords

Various Chords

Thirds

Sixths

B Major

Broken Chord

Interrupted Scale

Broken Chords

Returning Scales

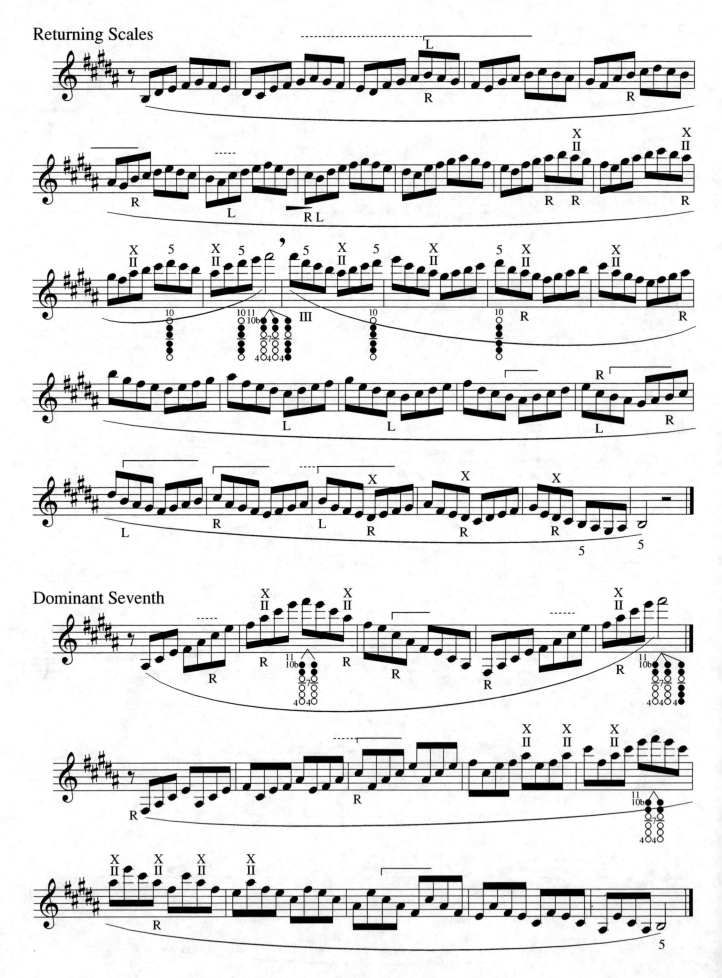

Dominant Seventh

(dominant seventh con't.)

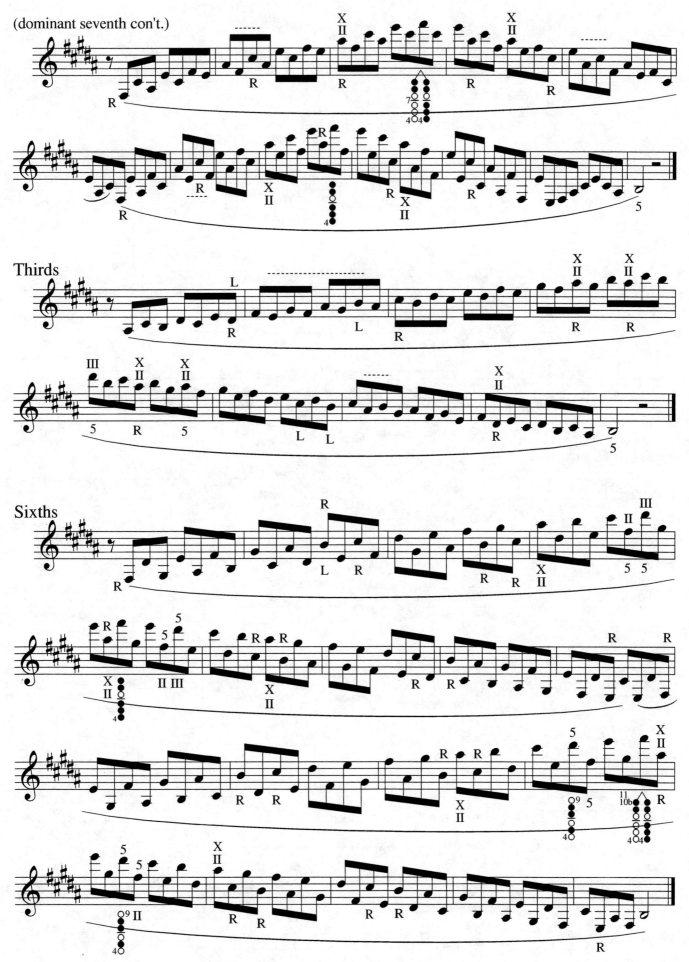

Thirds

Sixths

G# Minor

Melodic

Harmonic

Broken Chord

Returning Scales - Melodic

Harmonic

Broken Chords

Various Chords

Thirds

Sixths

D♭ Major

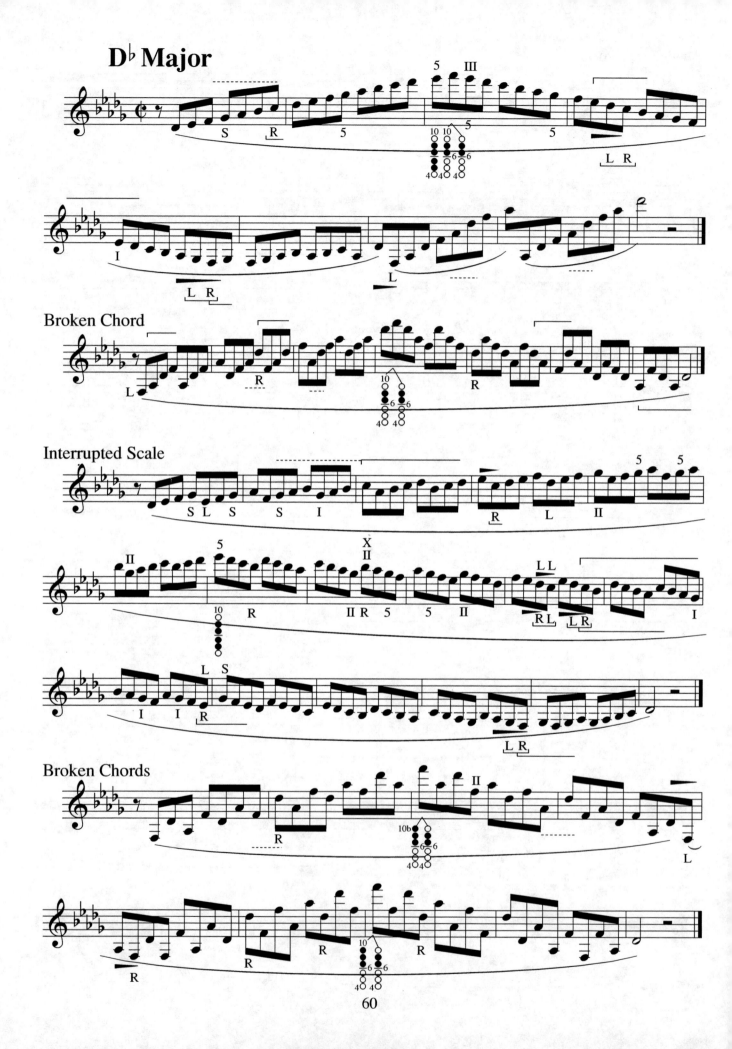

Broken Chord

Interrupted Scale

Broken Chords

60

Returning Scales

Dominant Seventh

61

Harmonic

Broken Chord

Interrupted Scales - Melodic

Harmonic

63

Broken Chords

Various Chords

Thirds

Sixths

G♭ **Major**

Broken Chord

Interrupted Scale

Broken Chords

65

Returning Scales

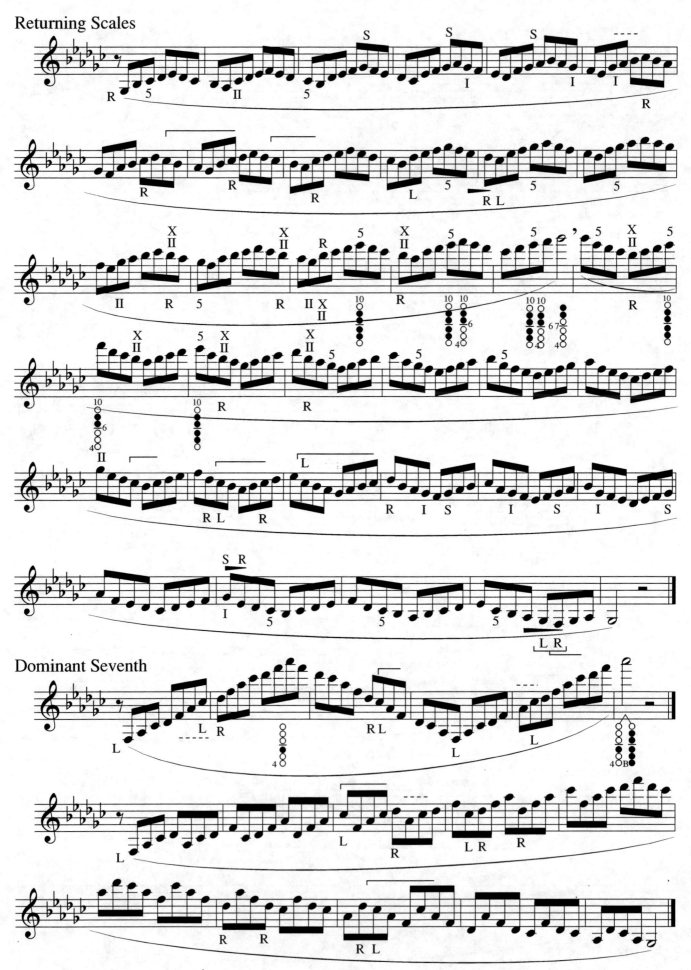

Dominant Seventh

Thirds

Sixths

67

E♭ Minor

Melodic

Harmonic

Broken Chord

Interrupted Scales - Melodic

Harmonic

68

69

Diminished Chords